T0130409

# God Counted to Ten

## Jill Blankenship

Copyright © 2023 Jill Blankenship.

All rights reserved. No part of this book may be used or reproduced by any means, graphic, electronic, or mechanical, including photocopying, recording, taping or by any information storage retrieval system without the written permission of the author except in the case of brief quotations embodied in critical articles and reviews.

WestBow Press books may be ordered through booksellers or by contacting:

WestBow Press
A Division of Thomas Nelson & Zondervan
1663 Liberty Drive
Bloomington, IN 47403
www.westbowpress.com
844-714-3454

Because of the dynamic nature of the Internet, any web addresses or links contained in this book may have changed since publication and may no longer be valid. The views expressed in this work are solely those of the author and do not necessarily reflect the views of the publisher, and the publisher hereby disclaims any responsibility for them.

Any people depicted in stock imagery provided by Getty Images are models, and such images are being used for illustrative purposes only. Certain stock imagery © Getty Images.

Interior Graphics/Art Credit: Jackie Shepherd

ISBN: 978-1-9736-9865-4 (sc)
ISBN: 978-1-9736-9866-1 (e)

Library of Congress Control Number: 2023909460

Print information available on the last page.

WestBow Press rev. date: 06/06/2023

WESTBOW
PRESS®
A DIVISION OF THOMAS NELSON
& ZONDERVAN

# God
# Counted
# to Ten

God told Moses to Pharaoh say,

"Let my people go"!


When Moses told Pharaoh,

Pharaoh said, "No"!

God turned water into blood.

When he counted to one.

God wanted to show Pharaoh.

What could be done.

God sent frogs,

when he counted to two

and

covered the whole land through.

When God counted to three
there were lice upon man.
God made them appear
from the dust of the land

When God counted to four

throughout Egypt flies did swarm.

God told Pharaoh this would happen.

To Pharaoh He did warn.

When God counted to five
Pharaoh did not obey.
The cattle of the Egyptians
died the next day.

Boils came upon all the people

when God counted to six.

It was a terrible thing,

that no man could fix.

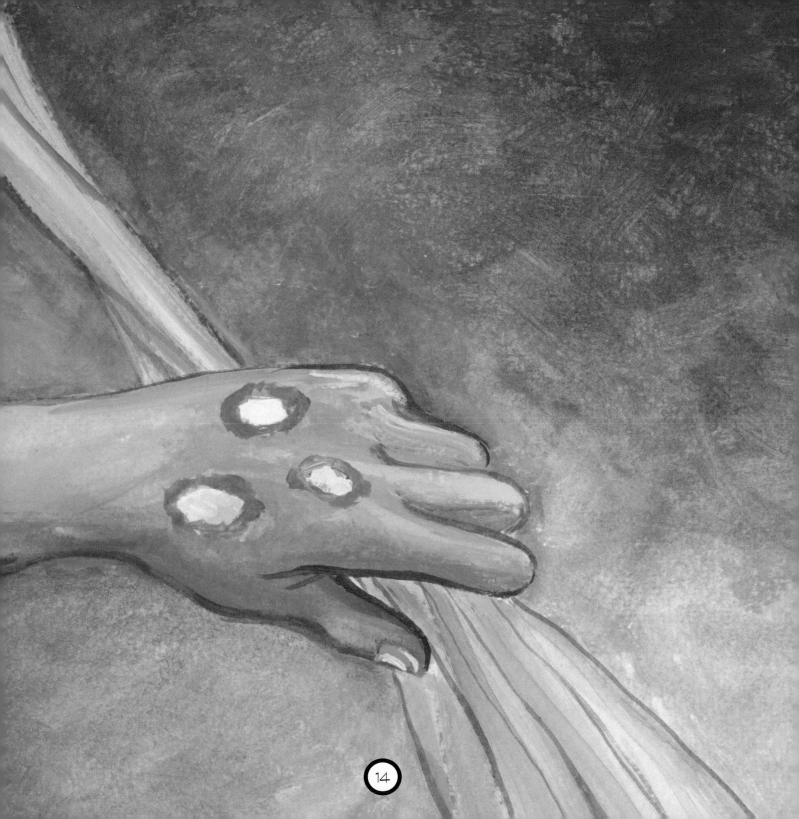

Pharaoh still refused to obey.

God counted to seven.

He sent hail across the land.

It rained down from Heaven.

After Pharaoh still said no.

God counted to eight.

He sent locusts upon the land.

The trees, the leaves and crops
they ate.

God counted to nine.

A great darkness covered the land.

It was so dark.

They could not see their hand.

At last, God counted to ten.

He said, "Let my people go"!

Pharoah still refused.

He still said, "No"!


God told him one last time.

Pharaoh still refused to obey.

God said the firstborn

would be taken away.

22

When God counted to ten.

Pharaoh chose to obey.

He let God's people go.

He told Moses to take them away.

Moses led God's people away
from Egypt that day.
God had listened and answered
the prayer they had prayed .

Printed in the United States
by Baker & Taylor Publisher Services